Etiquette for Success

Traveling Abroad

TITLES IN THE SERIES

Etiquette for Success

Traveling Abroad

Sarah Smith

MASON CREST

Mason Crest
450 Parkway Drive, Suite D
Broomall, Pennsylvania PA 19008
(866) MCP-BOOK (toll free)

First printing
9 8 7 6 5 4 3 2 1

ISBN: 978-1-4222-3975-9
Series ISBN: 978-1-4222-3969-8
ebook ISBN: 978-1-4222-7814-7

Printed and bound in the United States of America.

Library of Congress Cataloging-in-Publication Data

Names: Smith, Sarah (Freelance Writer), author.
Title: Traveling abroad / Sarah Smith.
Description: Broomall : Mason Crest, an imprint of National Highlights, Inc.,
  2018. | Series: Etiquette for success | Includes index.
Identifiers: LCCN 2018011620 (print) | LCCN 2018017321 (ebook) | ISBN
  9781422278147 (eBook) | ISBN 9781422239759 (hardback) | ISBN 9781422239698
  (series)
Subjects: LCSH: Travel etiquette.
Classification: LCC BJ2137 (ebook) | LCC BJ2137 .S65 2018 (print) | DDC
  395.5--dc23
LC record available at https://lccn.loc.gov/2018011620

QR CODES AND LINKS TO THIRD-PARTY CONTENT

Contents

KEY ICONS TO LOOK FOR:

 Words to Understand: These words with their easy-to-understand definitions will increase the reader's understanding of the text while building vocabulary skills.

 Sidebars: This boxed material within the main text allows readers to build knowledge, gain insights, explore possibilities, and broaden their perspectives by weaving together additional information to provide realistic and holistic perspectives.

 Educational Videos: Readers can view videos by scanning our QR codes, providing them with additional content to supplement the text. Examples include news coverage, moments in history, speeches, iconic sports moments, and much more!

 Text-Dependent Questions: These questions send the reader back to the text for more careful attention to the evidence presented there.

 Research Projects: Readers are pointed toward areas of further inquiry connected to each chapter. Suggestions are provided for projects that encourage deeper research and analysis.

 Series Glossary of Key Terms: This back-of-the-book glossary contains terminology used throughout the series. Words found here increase the reader's ability to read and comprehend higher-level books and articles in this field.

Introduction

Dear Reader,

As you read on, you will learn that in any given situation you must be knowledgeable about the expectations set by society regarding your actions and how they will or will not meet the social norms for good manners and etiquette.

It being essential to your success, you learn how your behavior will always be central to how others see you. Unfortunately, many people are judged, or written off almost instantly because of their lack of etiquette.

Times have certainly changed, and while society adapts, you must set your own goals for politeness, good manners, and kindness. All around you there are modern dilemmas to face, but let your good manners set you apart. Start by showing sensitivity toward others, maintain a keen awareness about how those around you feel, and note how your behavior impacts your peers.

Consider that even with changes in the world around you, etiquette must be inclusive and understanding across ages and cultures, and sensitive to your setting. It is important that you take the time to learn; read, practice, and ask questions of those whom you respect. Learn about writing a business letter, sending holiday invitations, or communicating with peers—certain etiquettes should be followed. Is it rude to keep checking your phone during lunch with a friend? Are handwritten thank-you notes still necessary?

It is said that good manners open doors that even the best education cannot. Read on and learn what it takes to make a great first impression.

"No duty is more urgent than that of returning thanks."

"No matter who you are or what you do, your manners will have a direct impact on your professional and social success."

"Respect for ourselves guides our morals; respect for others guides our manners"

"Life is short, but there is always time enough for courtesy"

Words to Understand

heritage: the traditions, achievements, and beliefs that are part of the history of a group of people

motivation: desire to do something; interest or drive

spiritual: relating to the spirit or soul and not to bodily or material matter

Traveling is a wonderful way of improving your perspective on life. It encourages resourcefulness and allows you to disconnect from your regular life. The memories created on your travels will be with you for a lifetime.

Chapter One
The Importance of Good Etiquette
in a Global World

What an exciting moment in history to be alive! At the touch of a button, you can access just about any information you want. You can travel across North America in less than about six hours and you can travel halfway around the world in a day. You can meet, work with, and befriend people from all different walks of life and spend time in places that will teach you as much about yourself as they will about different cultures and ethnicities. Make no mistake about it: traveling is a wonderful opportunity, and in today's modern age it's easier—and perhaps more important—than ever.

Why Should I Travel?

Humans are curious. It's in our nature to learn and try new things, both to fulfill our deep-rooted desires and to gain a sense of personal and perhaps **spiritual** growth. Travel is a powerful way to elicit these changes in yourself.

Maybe you want to travel to learn more about your **heritage**. Perhaps you want to meet new people or gain new experiences. Maybe you believe that you can make a positive difference in the world (hint: you *can*), so you view traveling as a way to spread your ideas and offer your help to others in need.

Maybe you're not even sure why you want to travel, you simply feel it deep inside as something you must do.

People who get the opportunity to travel far and wide are very fortunate. Nowadays, it is popular for students to travel during a gap year.

The Importance of Good Etiquette in a Global World

Whatever your **motivation**, know that you're not alone. Millions and millions of people travel every year, in large part due to (and sometimes in spite of) the growing trend toward global interconnectedness. Thanks to the Internet, communicating with people from all around the world is now as simple as typing a few words into your computer or dialing a number on your phone. We are able to connect with others in real time as local, national, and global changes occur all around us.

From political and civil unrest to exciting technological advances, environmental challenges, and more, there are literally thousands of events happening at any given moment and affecting every corner of our planet. For this reason, it's more helpful than ever to be comfortable and curious enough to travel—to be interested in both the history *and* future of our great planet.

How Should I Travel?

There are almost as many ways to travel around the world as there are places to go: solo, with friends, with family, with fellow students, with coworkers, with your boyfriend or girlfriend, or with volunteer programs. You may want to explore some or all of these travel methods over the course of your lifetime.

No matter which method you choose, it's important to be wise to the drawbacks as well as the benefits of traveling, which exist whether you're exploring your own hometown or if you've booked a one-way ticket to a country you've barely heard of.

Things like personal safety, respect for other cultures, and financial security are all important factors that the savvy traveler must be prepared to consider and account for during their vacations and holidays.

For this reason, bringing good etiquette along with you wherever you go is an extremely important aspect of successful traveling.

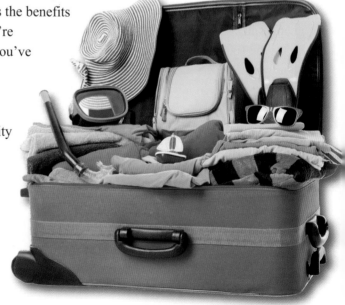

There are so many things to consider before you choose where to travel to. In summer, some countries are so hot that many tourists plan their trips during the winter or when it's cooler. This couple didn't check the weather statistics before they planned their trip!

The Importance of Good Etiquette in a Global World

Visiting incredible places, such as the Temples of Bagan in Myanmar (shown here), will provide you with wonderful memories and stories of your travels to take back home with you.

Etiquette, or the customary code of polite behaviors within a given society or community, will not only help you get more enjoyment out of your adventures but it will also help you stay safe and make a more positive impact on the people you meet and the places you go.

Having good etiquette helps make the world a better place, one brave and generous person at a time. And by striving to always present yourself in a kind, patient, tactful, and gracious manner, soon enough you'll have friends everywhere you go!

What to Expect From This Book

In this book, you're going to learn about what it means to travel with good etiquette—and why exactly it matters so much. It's not exactly a guide book full of cheap travel tips and top-secret destinations . . . instead, think of it as a "how-to" guide on traveling with poise, preparedness, class, and confidence.

We'll begin our journey by talking about things to consider relating to your specific mode or modes of transportation: how to get to where you're going, how to prepare for your travels, and what sort of paperwork and other logistical matters you'll need to take care of prior to your trip (depending on where you're headed).

Next up, you'll touch down in your destination of choice and learn about how to be respectful of other cultures and laws. You'll also see why making an effort to learn at least a little bit of a country's primary language can go a long way in terms of getting around safely and effectively.

Your safety, as well as the safety of your travel companions, should be your number one priority no matter where you go. Relying on information shared by some of the most respected global organizations and travel experts, this book highlights some of the most important things to consider when it comes to your physical health and financial means.

America is a large and diverse country with an extraordinary number of wonderful places to visit. The Grand Canyon National Park is in the top ten of places to visit in the United States.

The Importance of Good Etiquette in a Global World

For the less experienced, traveling in a group has many benefits. It is often more cost-effective, makes the trip easier and safer, and provides you with the opportunity to socialize with your companions.

Personal and financial safety is a nice segue into safety when it comes to meeting new people, especially in foreign countries. This book will give you some practical guidelines to help you develop meaningful relationships and enjoy positive interactions with all different types of people, while at the same time making sure that you maintain the necessary level of appropriateness, maturity, and safety.

Lastly, this book will help you prepare to put your best foot forward in any country you find yourself exploring by showing you ways to respectfully participate in its customs and traditions. Along the way, you'll also learn some interesting tidbits about global travel, including links to some amazing statistics, tips, and videos that you can use to prepare for your trip and wow your loved ones.

Seeing is believing, and experiencing a new place for yourself is a lot richer than simply reading about it in a book or on a website. So whether you already have a trip scheduled with your family or friends, are planning a solo adventure, or are simply dreaming of future travel destinations, buckle up: you're in for an exciting and eye-opening ride!

So clear your calendar and let's get going!

Text-Dependent Questions

1. If you travel by airplane, how many hours does it take to cross America?

2. Why is good etiquette important when visiting other countries?

3. How can learning the language of your destination country help you during your visit?

Research Project

Write a one-page essay on the benefits of traveling.

Words to Understand

passport: an official document issued by a government, certifying the holder's identity and citizenship and entitling them to travel under its protection to and from foreign countries

itinerary: a planned route or journey, or a travel document recording these

inoculations: vaccinations; medications (typically given via an injection) used to protect a person against disease or several diseases

Traveling abroad takes a good deal of planning. You will have to arrange travel documentation and tickets, currency, where to stay, inoculations, and many other things specific to the trip you have chosen.

Chapter Two
Preparing for Travel
by Air, Car & Rail:
Documents & Inoculations

Air, land, or sea: there's definitely more than one way to get out and see the world! Whether you're traveling by plane, train, bus, boat, or automobile, it's useful to brush up on some transportation-specific tips and suggestions that will help make sure your transit goes as smoothly as possible.

Pre-Trip To-Dos: A Handy Checklist

Don't let the excitement of your upcoming holiday or vacation distract you from some important logistical matters you will need to take care of before you go. There's nothing more frustrating or embarrassing than showing up at the airport with all your bags packed only to realize that you can't board the flight because you forgot your **passport** or made some other sort of oversight.

To make sure you prepare for your travel with attention to detail and organization, be certain to run through the following checklist well ahead of your departure date:

1. **Do Some Basic Research on the Place You're Headed.**
   Things you'll want to know include entry/exit requirements (including visas and **inoculations**), road safety and driving information, water safety, and the contact information of the nearest United States or Canadian embassy or consulate in case of emergency. You should also check if there are any travel warnings or alerts issued for the partof the world you're headed to; these

are intended to warn tourists of things such as wild weather, infrastructure problems, war and security issues, and disease outbreaks.

2. Prepare for Unexpected and Unlikely Emergencies.

Check with your health insurance plan to make sure you and your loved ones are covered while abroad. You may also want to consider buying supplemental insurance or emergency evacuation insurance, particularly if you are headed to a high-risk

> **Did You Know?**
>
> According to the International Air Transport Association, the world's first commercial airline flight flew on January 1, 1914, across Tampa Bay, Florida. The trip took twenty-three minutes and cost the single passenger, the mayor of St. Petersburg, about $400—which in today's money is equivalent to around $9,657!

part of the world. If you take medications, be sure to bring extra (at least five days' worth), and when you get to where you're going always have some clean bottled water on hand (either on your person or in the place you're staying).

3. Notify Your Bank and Credit Card Companies About Your Travel Plans.

A lot of major banks will put a freeze on your finances if they suddenly notice a charge made in a different country, or anything else that looks like unusual activity. You may also want to ask them and your cell phone provider about usage availability and fees for your phone, debit cards, use of ATMs, and so on.

Qantas Inflight Exercises

Keep Your Body Healthy When Flying

There are many ways to arrange your travel. Nowadays, you can either book through a traditional travel agent or online. Alternatively, you can book direct with a tour operator. Some people prefer to book each aspect of their trip separately, giving them more flexibility.

4. **Find Resources to Help Prepare for Special Considerations.**
   Certain Canadian and US citizens can expect to face some unique challenges when traveling abroad. This includes people who are female, LGBTI (lesbian, gay, bisexual, transgender, and intersex), senior adults, students, and journalists. Check official resources for information on how to be a safe and smart traveler, no matter what your individual situation.

Some Helpful Transportation Tips

- Traveling by plane? So are a lot of other people! Get to the airport at least two to three hours before your scheduled departure so you'll have plenty of time to get through security.

When passing through most international airports, you cannot take liquids of over 3.5 fl oz in your hand luggage. They must be kept in a clear plastic bag and separated from your other belongings when being scanned. This is an important measure used to combat terrorism.

- Keep an emergency roadside kit in your car that includes things like jumper cables, a flash light, and basic first aid supplies.
- Remember, most planes, trains, and buses have certain restrictions on things you can bring on board (e.g., liquids), so be sure to check with the travel company beforehand.
- Along with your important documents and medications, keep your phone charger, reading materials, important toiletries (including feminine products), a spare change of clothes, and some snacks in your carry-on bag. Chewing gum, for instance, can keep your ears from popping in a plane.
- Wear comfortable clothes, and avoid wearing strong perfume or cologne so as not to bother sensitive seatmates.
- Stay well hydrated. Drinking plenty of water will help you stay healthy, and will force you to frequently stand up or take breaks, which is important for joint and muscle health.

Don't Put Off Applying for Your Passport

According to information from both the Canadian and American governments, it typically takes anywhere from four to six weeks to obtain a passport, plus an additional one to three weeks for gathering, preparing, and sending in all the necessary information and fees. Even if you choose to pay extra for expedited service, you will still have to wait about two to three weeks for it. So be careful to apply for or renew your passport well in advance of your international travel. Once it arrives, keep it stored in a safe location—and don't forget to bring it with you when it's time to say *bon voyage*!

Important Paperwork to Bring When Traveling Abroad

You may not need all of the following paperwork. It really depends on the specific trip you're taking. Check with the airline or travel company you booked with. They will advise you on specific requirements relating to the country you are traveling to.

- Your passport and visas.
- Proof of health insurance and inoculations.
- Your travel **itinerary**, receipts and boarding passes (which may come from a travel agent, travel company, your airline, or may simply be a rough outline that you and your travel companions create). If you're using electronic tickets, you should write down the confirmation number in a notepad just in case.
- Contact information for the places where you'll be staying, as well as for your emergency contacts in your home country and at your destination.
- If applicable, a letter from your doctor listing the prescription medications you're carrying (if any) and the medical reason(s) why you need them (be sure to keep your medications in their original labeled containers).
- If applicable, any official letters from your company or school, or any organization that you're traveling with.
- Local currency, traveler's checks, and your debit and credit cards.

Prepare for Take-Off!

- An estimated 8 million people fly in airplanes every day.

- The FAA handles approximately 44,000 flights daily.

- There are approximately 19,500 airports in the United States.

Most travelers take to flying easily. There is something very exciting about taking off from your home country and then flying to somewhere else both different and exotic.

Whatever you end up bringing with you, be sure to keep your documents safely secured with you or a trusted travel companion at all times (or locked in a safe in your hotel room, for instance). You should *never* put important documents in your checked baggage, or leave them unsecured and unsupervised for any reason.

Before you depart, be sure to make color photocopies of all of your paperwork, especially your passport, visas, and itinerary. Someone you trust at home should get a copy of these documents (feel free to seal them in an envelope for privacy). You should also bring a copy of your passport with you, but keep this stored securely and separately from where you're keeping your actual passport.

Text-Dependent Questions

1. How many people are estimated to fly by airplane each day?

2. Name three important documents you should bring with you on an international trip.

3. You should make two copies of your passport when you travel abroad. What should you do with each of them?

Research Project

Visit the website **http://travel.state.gov/content/passports/en/country.html** (if you're in the United States), or **https://wwwnc.cdc.gov/travel/destinations/list** (if you're in Canada), then use it to do some research about a country you'd like to visit. Do you need any visas or inoculations to visit this country? Are there specific entry/exit restrictions? Are there are any current travel warnings or alerts for that area? Write a one- to two-page report summarizing your findings.

Words to Understand

ambassador: a person who acts as a representative or promoter of a specified activity

culture: the customs, arts, social institutions, and achievements of a particular nation, people, or other social group

assimilate: become absorbed by or accepted into a community or culture

Sightseeing buses are a cost-effective way of exploring a city. You can usually hop on and off whenever you need to and there is invariably a recorded travel commentary you can plug earphones into.

Chapter Three
——— Respecting Other ———
Cultures, Communities & Laws

When you go abroad, imagine yourself as an **ambassador** of your home country. Not only are you representing yourself but you are also representing your own nation. One of the best ways to be a socially conscious traveler and represent yourself and your nation well is to show respect for the **culture** and laws of the places you're visiting. After all, foreign countries are likely to be at least a *little* different from your own . . . and in some cases they may be drastically different! Exposing yourself to these novel experiences can help you become a more open-minded and culturally sensitive person, which will not only enrich your travel experiences but can also give you some important advantages when it comes to your future academic and career opportunities.

Of course, you don't have to memorize a country's entire legal system in order to travel there with class and civility, but it's never a bad idea to do a little research before your trip. Consider searching the web for some reputable travel blogs written by people who have traveled to where you're headed. What's been other tourists' experiences? Are there any official websites, books, or other resources to help you get a better understanding of what to expect when you arrive?

Top Dos & Don'ts of Being a Law-Abiding Traveler

DO brush up on local laws. Certain countries, for instance, require women to cover their heads in public places. Others may have curfews, prohibitions against texting while driving, laws against feeding wildlife, and restrictions against foreign drivers.

DO ask questions. Many local folks enjoy helping tourists learn about their culture. Rely on your tour guide, waiter, taxi driver,

Respecting Other Cultures, Communities & Laws

hotel staff, local police, host family, friends who have traveled before, or anyone else you come across on your travels for tips and information.

DO try to learn (and use) at least a few key words and phrases in the country's native language (more on this in the next chapter).

DO know your boundaries as a foreign participant. Observing or getting involved in a foreign ceremony or ritual can be a good way to show your curiosity and reverence for another person's culture. But you should only plan on doing this if you are explicitly invited to participate, especially if it is a religious service. This is because you may end up doing something disrespectful without even realizing it. Understand that many cultural ceremonies and practices are considered sacred, and should be treated as such.

DON'T assume that just because something is legal or socially acceptable in your home country it will also be legal or socially acceptable in the country you're visiting.

DON'T be rude if someone points out something you're doing that is frowned upon or even illegal. Yes, it may be embarrassing, but see it as a learning opportunity that will help you grow into a more mature and considerate world traveler.

DON'T fall into the trap of "if everybody does it, it must be okay." When it comes to having good etiquette, being a leader for your travel companions instead of a follower can make a world of difference, literally and figuratively.

DON'T be afraid to try new foods! This is a huge one. Eating ethnic cuisine is a great way to **assimilate** yourself into the local culture. You don't have like everything you try, of course, but you should stay polite and open-minded. Who knows . . . you may end up finding a new favorite dish!

Showing Respect to Indigenous People

The most popular tourist attractions in many countries are near and dear to the local indigenous people. You want to tread lightly on these areas—literally—and keep in mind that just because it's not necessarily *illegal* to do something doesn't mean that it's not culturally insensitive either. For instance, the famous Australian monolith known as Uluru, or Ayers Rock, has a significant spiritual and cultural significance to the local Aboriginal people. While tourists are not prohibited from climbing the structure, local tribe members ask that visitors stay off of it, as it's considered highly disrespectful (and may actually be damaging to the ancient structure itself).

"Leave No Trace"

In addition to following the above dos and don'ts, you should also abide by the classic hiking creed of "Leave no trace." Many outdoor experts consider this your number one obligation while you are spending time in nature, and it applies wherever you are around the world. Leaving no trace allows everyone to see and enjoy nature while minimizing negative impacts caused by humans. In addition, when you demonstrate these principles it shows your travel companions and the local people that you are respectful of the culture, geography, and country.

Here are the seven key principles of "Leave no trace," as described by the American organization Leave No Trace Center for Outdoor Ethics:

When visiting religious sights, such as the temple shown here, make sure you check the dress code before you go, as if you are not appropriately dressed, you may cause offense or may not be allowed to enter.

Respecting Other Cultures, Communities & Laws

The Seven Principles of Leave No Trace

While Muslim countries such as Dubai open their doors to vacationers, they have strict codes of conduct that must be adhered to and studied before travel. In Dubai, behavior that is legal in the West, for example drinking alcohol outside specific areas or holding hands in a public place, is illegal.

- Plan ahead and prepare
- Travel and camp on durable surfaces
- Dispose of waste properly
- Leave what you find
- Minimize campfire impacts
- Respect wildlife
- Be considerate of other visitors

Of course, the concept of leaving no trace doesn't only apply to outdoor travel. This "duty of the traveler" can also be extended to whenever you are visiting an urban area, or even staying in a host family's home. Be tidy, be neat, and be clean: it's a way to show respect for yourself and the country you're in.

Text-Dependent Questions

1. Why is it important to be a socially conscious traveler?

2. Name two dos and don'ts about showing respect for a country's laws and unique culture as a tourist.

3. Should you climb Uluru (Ayers Rock) in Australia? Why or why not?

Research Project

Once again, the website **http://travel.state.gov/content/passports/en/country.html** (if you're in the United States), or **https://wwwnc.cdc.gov/travel/destinations/list** (if you're in Canada), is useful for finding out specific customs of a destination country. You already saw this site in the previous chapter about documentation and trip preparation. This time, do some research and write an essay on your findings about specific laws and customs in a different country you'd like to visit. Include some basic information, such as primary languages, main religions, and important local laws. In particular, focus on laws that may pertain to you or other loved ones as tourists. Are there any specific rules or restrictions for people who are LGBTI, followers of particular religions, journalists, senior citizens, and so on?

Words to Understand

fluent: able to speak or write a particular foreign language easily and accurately

immersion: a method of teaching a foreign language by the exclusive use of that language, usually at a special school

repertoire: all the things that a person is able to do

When traveling to a foreign-language country, those who have mastered the language have a distinct advantage, especially if they become lost and need to ask directions from someone.

Chapter Four
The Importance of
Learning Other Languages

Aside from religion, language is probably the most important thread of any culture. In fact, many schools and study abroad programs use total **immersion** as a way to quickly and comprehensively help students learn a new language and thereby become familiar with a new country.

While it can be intimidating to travel in a place where you don't know the main languages, this shouldn't be a reason to avoid visiting these places. After all, even though English isn't spoken everywhere you go, it's entirely possible to see and learn a lot about a new place, and get around safely, without being **fluent** in the local language.

Instead, consider "hacking" your language learning by memorizing a few key phrases, words, and expressions beforehand. Do you know a native speaker personally? Be sure to practice with them before your trip!

Helpful Terms & Phrases to Know in the Primary Language of Your Travel Destination

"Hello"
Greeting someone in their own language makes you seem approachable, friendly, and engaged. Learn the polite way to say

The Importance of Learning Other Languages

If you lose your way in a city and need to ask for help, a taxi driver is often a good source of information. He will invariably know all the names of the streets and the locations of the major tourist destinations.

hi to someone in a foreign language, and realize that in certain languages you have to say "Hello" in a different way depending on who you're talking to (for example, someone older than you versus someone younger than you). Other helpful greeting phrases to know include "Excuse me," "My name is," and "Goodbye."

"Do You Speak English?"

Usually, asking this question won't come off as rude, and if the person you're talking to can communicate in your primary language it may save both of you a bit of time and headache. That said, don't be disappointed or rude if they say no . . . and don't be tempted to only speak in English the whole time you're traveling!

To help ease your nervousness, and hopefully help the other person feel a little more patient with you, consider learning and using the phrase, "I speak a little bit of . . ." or "I am learning . . ." followed by whatever language you're speaking in (e.g., "I speak a little bit of Spanish" or "I am learning Russian").

"Please"

Basic etiquette at it's finest: "Please" and "Thank you"! Learn these phrases, learn them well, and be prepared to use them often. You should also research other common courtesy phrases, including "No thank you," "I'm sorry," and "I don't understand."

"Where is . . . ?"

This is helpful when asking for directions. Gestures and maps can help (but remember that in some countries it may be considered rude to point!).

Everyday Items

Having a few common words in your personal **repertoire** can make things a lot easier for you as you go about your day in a foreign country. Consider memorizing some words that you plan on using a lot and that can help you

The Ten Most Commonly Spoken Languages in the World

Think English is the world's most common language? Think again! According to the popular language learning app Babbel, the top ten spoken languages (including their subdialects, where applicable) from around the globe are Chinese, Spanish, English, Hindi, Arabic, Portuguese, Bengali, Russian, Japanese, and Punjabi.

Try learning a language as part of your daily routine. There are plenty of free apps to choose from including Duolingo, busuu, Babbel, and Memrise.

The Importance of Learning Other Languages

Anyone Can Learn a Language

Before you travel to a foreign-language country, consider downloading a translation app. They are very useful for translating road signs, menus, phrases, and other written matter.

communicate your basic needs, such as "bathroom," "water," "coffee," "food," "computer," "Internet," or the numbers one to ten.

Important Tips for Traveling in a Foreign-Language Country

Don't be hard on yourself! Almost everybody needs a lot of practice and exposure to a language before they gain even basic conversational fluency. And while you shouldn't expect people around you to speak English perfectly (if at all), you also shouldn't expect to speak the foreign language yourself perfectly either.

That's a Lot of Language

According to Ethnologue, a worldwide language database, there are an estimated 7,099 known living languages currently in existence. It's difficult to get an exact number, since there is some debate about distinct languages versus subdialects. That said, of these 7,000+ recognized languages, some have over 1 billion native speakers (such as Chinese), while some have fewer than 1,000!

Rely on locals for help. Many languages use sounds, pronunciations, and other verbal expressions that may be pretty unfamiliar to you and awkward for you to say. If you're not sure you're saying something correctly, just ask! The phrase "How do you say . . . ?" can be useful to facilitate this exchange: simply ask "How do you say . . . ?" in the person's language, followed by the phrase that you're trying to pronounce. If you are speaking with someone who speaks English as well as the language that's new to you, you can also say "How do you say . . . ?" followed by the word in English, thus giving you a chance to learn more foreign vocabulary!

Jot down your key phrases in a journal

The Importance of Learning Other Languages

Once you have mastered the basics of learning a foreign language at school or college, it is beneficial to then plan a trip to a country where your newly learned language is spoken. This will improve your ability and boost your confidence in the language.

and keep this with you. You may also want to note them down on your phone (assuming you are planning to use your phone internationally). You may want to write these words phonetically (written how they sound) so you will remember how to pronounce them correctly. This is particularly useful in languages that use different letters or symbols than the standard English alphabet you're probably used. For example, Спасибо means "Thank you" in Russian, but it sounds like "spa-see-ba" so you may want to write that instead.

If you or someone you are traveling with has special needs or a certain medical condition, is traveling for a specific reason, or if you anticipate that you may have to deal with any sort of complicated situation frequently, consider writing down complete sentences in the new language. In this case, you'll need to spell the words correctly so locals can read it. By doing so, you can simply show the card to the person you're communicating with, while being less concerned about miscommunication. If you use this method, be sure to also show respect by also speaking those common courtesy phrases like "Please" and "Thank you."

Text-Dependent Questions

1. Name two or three basic phrases or words you should know in any language.

2. When traveling in a foreign-language country, why is it useful to write down some key phrases in a notebook in case you need them?

3. Name three of the top ten spoken languages in the world. What rank is English?

Research Project

Think of a foreign-language country you would love to visit. Then learn and memorize the following phrases: "Hello," "My name is . . . ," "Thank you," "Please," and "Goodbye." Consider learning how to write and say these words.

Words to Understand

exchange rate: the value of one currency for the purpose of conversion to another

tchotchke: a small object that is decorative rather than strictly functional; a trinket

pickpockets: people who steal from other people's pockets

Currencies		WE BUY	WE SELL
Euro	EUR	1.4957	
USA	USD	1.6340	
Australia	AUD	2.2392	1.9398
South Africa	ZAR		21.9751

A Bureau de Change is a place where foreign currencies are exchanged. The most common currencies such as the US dollar and the euro can usually be bought and supplied immediately. However, some of the less-common currencies have to be ordered a few days earlier.

Chapter Five
Money & Staying
Safe Abroad

B eing in a foreign country poses a lot of unique challenges, and minding your money and your personal safety are two of the most critical things you need to pay attention to every day of your trip. While it's not possible to completely eliminate your chances of being taken advantage of by unsavory and dishonest people, there are many things you can do to reduce your risk.

Smart Money Tips for the Savvy Traveler

Give Your Bank a Heads-Up

Remember, before traveling out of the country, let your bank know about your trip, too. If you live in America and your bank then suddenly sees a charge to your account made in India, this will trigger a fraud alert and they may end up freezing your funds until further action from you—which is definitely a headache you want to avoid if possible.

Don't Over-Pack!

Airplanes charge extra for overstuffed bags. Know weight restrictions before you fly, and only pack things that you really want and will use (hint: you usually need far less than you think).

Be Prepared to Use Cash

Although it's possible in most countries to use debit or credit cards (Visa and Mastercard being the most common), it's helpful and often easier to be able to use the local currency from time to time, especially for smaller day-to-day purchases. While some people recommend getting foreign currency before you arrive in your destination, it may

Don't forget to spend your coins. Invariably, you cannot exchange them for dollars when you get home. While away, familiarize yourself with their value, so you can confidently count out the change and not hand over another note.

actually be cheaper to wait until you arrive at the airport or find an ATM (postal banks inside post offices are also usually cheaper options). Just be sure to ask your bank in advance if there will be any foreign transaction fees for withdrawing money from an ATM; if there are, you may want to take out as much as you need at one time to minimize multiple withdrawal charges.

Hint: foreign coins often end up getting lost or going to waste when you come home, so be sure to spend these if you have them (think: postcards, coffees, etc.).

Don't Be Afraid to Double- and Triple-Check Your Change

It's not uncommon to be shortchanged by a vendor sometimes, whether accidentally or on purpose (unfortunately). Pay attention to how much money you're getting back, and be sure

Watch Out for Roaming Charges

Most cell phone carriers charge a fee for what's known as "international roaming." These vary from country to country and can be a costly expense. Your carrier will be able to supply details. Alternatively, you may want to consider buying an international SIM card.

to study the coins and bills closely enough so that you can comfortably identify them.

Know the Exchange Rates

Once you familiarize yourself with the local money, try to keep a rough estimate of the **exchange rate** between your home country's currency and the foreign currency in mind. This way, it'll be easier for you to know how much you're spending wherever you go. Some people also opt to use cash conversion applications on their smartphones, which can be a great option provided that your phone works overseas.

Pay Attention to Your Spending Habits

Do you *really* want that **tchotchke**? Are you buying that little trinket because you actually love it, or is it more of an impulse buy?

Spending money on gifts can really add up on a trip. While you should feel free to use your hard-earned money the way you see fit, many travel experts will tell you that putting more of your money toward experiences (e.g., meals, event tickets, outdoor excursions, museum passes) rather than things usually makes for a more memorable and meaningful way to see the world.

Nowadays, our cell phone has become part of everyday life. When traveling, however, it is a vital piece of safety equipment that means you can be in touch with your folks at home or emergency services within seconds.

Money & Staying Safe Abroad

A well-secured money belt is a very useful piece of equipment for keeping your cash and other valuables safe. When worn under clothes, it is virtually invisible. This is a good alternative to carrying a bag, which can either be mislaid or snatched. While most places are relatively safe places to visit, some large cities are known for pickpockets, so in this case a money belt is essential.

Smart Traveling Tips
for Travelers

This is also another reason why paying for things in cash can be a good idea, since it helps you keep track of how much money you're actually spending. That way, you'll come home with lots of memories instead of lots of silly souvenirs and credit card debt or empty pockets!

Top Tips for Staying Safe While Abroad

Personal safety is right up there with financial smarts, and the reality is that there are people out there that enjoy taking advantage of seemingly naive tourists. Here are some of the most important things to do to stay safe in a foreign country:

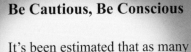

Be Cautious, Be Conscious

It's been estimated that as many as 400,000 incidences of pickpocketing occur every day around the world. What are some of the worst cities in the world for pickpockets? Barcelona, Rome, and Paris.

In some countries, tourists can be targets for thieves. Leaving valuables, such as purses, cameras, jewelery, etc., on show can attract the wrong kind of attention. Keep valuable items concealed or leave them in the hotel safe.

43

Money & Staying Safe Abroad

- Always let your friends or family members know your plans and where you're headed when going out.
- Write down the name of your accommodation in a notebook (don't rely only on a note in your phone, since batteries can die!) or memorize it. If necessary, jot it down in English and in the local language. This way, you'll be able to ask for directions if you ever get lost.
- Use hotel safes to store your valuables. Consider leaving some cash and an extra credit or debit card in there, too. Depending on where you are and what you're doing, you may not even need to bring your passport with you everywhere you go, so consider leaving that locked up, too.

Traveling abroad is a great way of meeting new people and making friends. However, regardless of whether you are male or female, stay safe by being alert, be aware of your surroundings, and use your common sense.

- Pay attention to your surroundings, especially while walking at night or alone. Don't fiddle with your phone or purse as you walk, and keep your personal items close to you and with you at all times. If you find yourself walking alone at night, stay on well-lit streets and try to walk near couples or other people. Better yet, don't walk alone at all—stay with your group. Be suspicious of potential **pickpockets**.
- Don't do anything that will draw unnecessary attention to yourself. This is good etiquette and good common sense. For instance, try not to do anything that appears "obviously" touristy (like being overly reliant on selfie-sticks, keeping your nose buried in a map, or not protecting your bag or purse). You should also avoid wearing overly revealing clothing (especially if the local culture or laws prohibit it) or appearing (let alone becoming) too drunk.
- Never leave a drink unattended.
- Trust your instincts. If you think you're being followed or are uncomfortable for any reason, slip into a public place (e.g., restaurant, hotel lobby, police station) and ask for help—do not keep walking to where you're headed.

Text-Dependent Questions

1. Should you let your bank know that you are traveling abroad before you leave the country? Why or why not?

2. Name three things that you can do to stay safe when traveling abroad.

3. How many pickpocket incidents are estimated to occur every day around the world?

Research Project

Come up with a list of ten foreign countries that you would like to visit. Then look up the current exchange rate between the currency of these countries and your own country.

Words to Understand

ethnicities: beliefs, customs, arts, etc., of particular societies or groups

hostel: an establishment that provides inexpensive food and lodging for a specific group of people, such as students, workers, or travelers

homestay: a popular form of hospitality and lodging whereby visitors stay in the house or apartment of a local person in the city they are visiting

Making friends on vacation is a wonderful way of learning about the cultures of other countries. Once you return home, it's easy to stay in touch using social media, the telephone, and good old-fashioned letter writing.

Chapter Six
Making Friends & Forming Relationships Abroad

W e travel the world to experience new things and learn more about ourselves. We also travel to meet other people and gain a better understanding of the similarities and differences between various cultures and **ethnicities**.

Wherever you go, getting to know the local people should be one of your main travel goals. It's a great way to gain a deeper understanding of the country's culture, plus you may discover some amazing and lesser-known places to visit as a tourist.

Meeting new people while traveling can be a bit nerve-racking, especially if you're in a foreign country and haven't mastered the language. Fortunately, there are plenty of ways you can get to know the locals without having to rely only on establishments like bars or dance clubs.

Clever Ways to Meet Locals & Fellow Travelers When Exploring Abroad

From baristas to butchers, the local folks in any town around the world have a lot of wisdom and stories to share, so keep an open mind! If the thought of introducing yourself and meeting new people (perhaps even other travelers from different parts of the world) seems a bit intimidating, keep the following suggestions in mind:

• Check out social media. Sharing your upcoming holiday plans with your Facebook friends may help you connect with people who live in the area you're visiting, or who themselves are visiting. Mutual connections make for great resources

Meet Up with Meetup

https://www.meetup.com allows you to connect with local clubs and groups in almost any corner of the world. Browse gatherings and outings based on location and interest. Alternatively, InterNations (https://www.internations.org) connects people internationally.

for ride-sharing, travel partners, and more. You can also type in the name of the town you'll be heading to and search for nearby events to attend. Scrolling through Twitter and Instagram feeds for hashtags related to your area can also help you find out about local events and see what other tourists are up to.

- Become a creature of habit. If you're staying in a foreign place for an extended period of time (such as for a study abroad program), try developing a few regular habits, such as going for a morning walk or stopping to read and use the Internet at the local library. Having a routine can make you more likely to see the same people more than once, which may pique their interest in you and make it seem easier to strike up a conversation.

- Sign up for guided tours. Tours are a great way to see more of a city you don't know and learn about it from someone who is highly knowledgeable. Plus, it's an easy way to meet other like-minded people who share similar interests. Don't be surprised to find that many of your fellow tour-group members may actually be locals themselves who are vacationing as "tourists" in their own country or region.

- Volunteer or join a group. Sports or language-learning groups at your foreign university, community service groups in the town, or dance or yoga classes at local gyms are all

Tips on Staying in a Hostel

If you plan to stay abroad for a prolonged period and wish to meet new people, joining a gym, dance, or yoga class will make it easier to make friends.

excellent ways to meet new people without having to worry about the awkward task of finding something in common to talk about.

- Attend local sporting events. There's hardly anything more universal than competition. Plus, many locals will enjoy teaching you about the foreign sport and getting you interested in the game or match.

When we are away from home for a long time, some of us start to miss our folks back home. By using apps such as Skype and Facetime, you can connect with your loved ones at any time of day or night.

- Consider alternative accommodations. Hotels are nice but they're not always great places to meet other people. Smaller, more community-minded accommodations such as a **hostel**, Airbnb, Couchsurfing, or a **homestay**, can instead help connect you with people your own age and locals who are willing to share insights into their homeland.
- Do as the locals do. Is there a favorite coffee hotspot near your hotel? What about a park, farmer's market, or outdoor festival? Ask your hotel or hostel staff about any local events and be sure to check them out with your buddies.
- People who travel can make lasting friendships and even intimate partnerships with others from literally anywhere on Earth. Thanks to modern technology, it's now easier than ever to keep in touch with your worldwide friends. So while you should always maintain a level of street smarts about you, try not to be shy about meeting other people when traveling. You never know where your new connections will take you!

Text-Dependent Questions

1. What is a hostel?

2. List three different ways you can meet a fellow traveler or local while traveling abroad.

3. Name two things you can do to show your appreciation and respect for your host when you're a house guest.

Research Project

Think of a foreign city that you'd love to visit. Then do some research on interesting ways you could meet locals or other tourists there. Consider using websites like Facebook, Twitter, Meetup.com, or the city's tourist webpage.

Words to Understand

custom: a traditional and widely accepted way of behaving or doing something that is specific to a particular society, place, or time

taboo: a social or religious custom prohibiting or forbidding discussion of a particular practice or forbidding association with a particular person, place, or thing

geopolitical: relating to politics, especially international relations, as influenced by geographical factors

Some countries have very strict religious laws that have to be respected by everyone. If you are in doubt about a country's code of conduct, do thorough research on the subject prior to traveling there.

Chapter Seven
Understanding the Customs of Other Countries

In this book, you've learned about how and why you should be mindful of other countries' laws and cultures. To finish up your around-the-world lesson in etiquette, this chapter will point out a few things to consider when learning about, exploring, or even adopting a country's customs.

You may be wondering what the difference is between culture and **custom**. Perhaps the easiest way to think about these important concepts is this: customs help define a country's culture. Customs are the norms, rituals, or taboos practiced or upheld by *individuals* in a society, and which form a key part of a particular culture, whereas culture refers to *groups of individuals* (sometimes the population of an entire country) and covers things like beliefs, laws, and values as well as customs. A nation or society's culture depends not only on its customs, however, but also on other factors, including its beliefs, morals, and so on.

So showing respect for another country's culture by trying to learn more about it, by learning the language, and getting to know the locals is important if you want to have good etiquette while traveling. But by understanding the local customs and traditions, you will really be able to establish yourself as a tactful and worldly person.

It is wonderful to experience other cultures and customs. By being respectful and understanding, you will be able to establish yourself as a worldly and courteous person.

53

Understanding the Customs of Other Countries

In some countries, such as Thailand for example, edible insects are deep fried until crisp and then salted. Throughout Thailand, carts in the streets are piled high with freshly cooked bugs on sale. In recent years, eating a bag full of these bugs has become a tradition for tourists. Beware though, some are a little scary looking!

A Guide to Table Manners From Around the World

Important Customs and Traditions to Learn About Different Countries

Meals and Tipping

What time do you eat dinner: six o'clock or nine o'clock? This may depend on what country you're in, and not just how hungry you are!

Meals are sometimes small and short in certain cultures. In others, a meal can last for hours and appear in stages, spread out over many different courses (e.g., hole-in-the-wall eateries for dinner in Tokyo vs. French dégustation menu).

Many Cultures, Many Customs

https://www.commisceo-global.com/country-guides offers country culture guides for anyone looking to gain special insight into what makes different countries unique. Topics range from food to business practices to favorite pastimes.

Other dining considerations you should learn about include:

- Whether or not it's acceptable to ask for second helpings
- What type of utensils are used and how to use them
- Country-specific table manners (e.g., burping, slurping food, eating with your hands, or putting elbows on the table)
- Whether tipping the wait staff is expected, and if so, how much is deemed appropriate
- Be willing to eat a meal in the traditional way of the particular culture you're in, and enjoy the experience.

Drinking Age and Attitudes

Alcohol can be a contentious point in different cultures. In some countries (like Afghanistan and Indonesia) alcohol is a major **taboo**. These places tend to have strict regulations or prohibitions against

French cuisine is considered to be one of the finest in the world. When in France, visiting a good restaurant should be on everyone's list.

Understanding the Customs of Other Countries

alcohol. In other countries, however, the consumption of alcohol is an important part of cultural and family tradition. In France, for instance, it's not unusual for young children to have small sips of wine at mealtimes when dining with their families.

Take care to know the legal drinking age of the country you're in, which will typically range from sixteen to twenty-one years old. If you're above the legal drinking age, then feel free to enjoy alcoholic beverages responsibly. For your safety and health, however, you should avoid getting too drunk.

Driving and Getting Around

How do people get around in the country you're visiting? Some cities, like Copenhagen and Amsterdam, are known for being extremely bike-friendly, for instance. In other places, like Italy, mopeds can be seen on many city streets. Taking public transportation or simply

Many cities around the world are bike-friendly. Bikes are a great way of getting around and can usually be hired out.

walking may also be great choices if you want to get a better feel for the unique culture of your destination.

If you're thinking about driving in a different country, realize that certain traffic laws may be different, including right-of-way, roundabout rules, and which side of the road you're supposed to drive on! You should also check with your car insurance company and the country's official government website to find out if it's even legal for you to operate any sort of motorized vehicle, including mopeds. Your home driving licence may not be valid in a foreign country, so check before you leave and apply for an international licence if necessary.

Nap Time!

Perhaps one of the most well-known customs of Spain and certain other countries is the traditional afternoon siesta, a time during which businesses shut down and people relax with friends and family, take long lunches, or take an actual nap. Traditionally, they have served to help people avoid the hottest part of the day, but the practice of siestas has changed over time.

Work and Business

How long is the typical work day? What kind of value and honor is placed on careers and industry? Japan, for instance, has an incredibly demanding workplace culture, whereas other cultures are known for being much more laid-back.

If you're thinking about volunteering or working overseas, remember that you should check with the country to find out what sort of visas or special clearances you may need.

Religious Customs, Family Traditions, and Interpersonal Interactions

If you can, consider staying with a host family while you are abroad. There is hardly a better way to learn about a culture's deep-rooted customs than to live with a local family. Your host parents and siblings can teach you about special traditions around holidays, family birthdays, and other important events. They can also teach you about socially acceptable ways to interact and communicate with strangers you meet in public.

Remember that you should not expect to participate in religious ceremonies unless asked or invited to do so.

Sports and Leisure

How do the locals like to relax? What sports are their favorite to watch on television? Everything from saunas to bocce ball or espresso bars is worth experiencing!

Understanding the Customs of Other Countries

Once you have traveled in your own country or visited a few new countries, your confidence will have grown enormously, so that next time you plan a trip, you can go further away or even off the beaten track.

Travel Often, Travel Well

By now, you're hopefully starting to feel a lot more confident about worldwide travel. Our planet is an amazing place, and the more people explore and learn about it, the more connected and understanding we'll be with each other. And what better time is there to do this than now?

At a moment in history when vast and important changes are occurring in virtually every realm of society (**geopolitical**, economic, environmental, technological, and social), having new generations of young people who understand how to be savvy and sensitive when traveling will truly be able to make a world of difference.

Text-Dependent Questions

1. What is the difference between culture and custom?

2. Name two aspects of a country's customs that you should learn more about before you visit.

3. What is a siesta?

Research Project

Revisit the webpage http://www.commisceo-global.com/country-guides and look up information about two countries you'd love to visit. Write a one- to two-page summary of the most interesting customs in each.

Series Glossary of Key Terms

appreciation	Gratitude and thankful recognition.
body language	Nonverbal communication through posture or facial expression.
bully	Overbearing person who habitually intimidates weaker or smaller people.
civil	Adhering to the norms of polite social intercourse.
clingy	Tending to stay very close to someone for emotional support.
common sense	Sound judgment based on simple perceptions of a situation.
compatible	Capable of existing together in harmony.
compliment	An expression of affection, respect, or admiration.
confidence	The state of being certain.
cyberbullying	The electronic posting of mean-spirited messages about a person.
empathy	Being aware of the feelings and thoughts of another.
eulogy	A commendatory oration or writing, especially in honor of one deceased.
faux pas	A social blunder.
frenemy	One who pretends to be a friend but is actually an enemy.
gossip	A person who habitually reveals personal facts about others.
grace	Disposition to act with kindness and courtesy.
inappropriate	Not suited for a purpose or situation.
initiative	The power to do something before others do.
inoculation	Injecting a vaccine to protect against or treat disease.
integrity	The quality of being honest and fair.
judgmental	Tending to judge people too quickly and critically.
lust	To have an intense desire or need.
manner	The way something is done or happens.
networking	The cultivation of productive relationships.
peer	One who is of equal standing with another.
poise	A natural, self-confident manner.
polite	Having or showing good manners or respect for others.
prioritize	To organize things so that the most important one is dealt with first.
procrastinate	To put off intentionally and habitually.
problem-solving	The process of finding a solution to a problem.
online	Connected to a computer.
relationship	The way in which two or more people are connected.
respect	To consider worthy of high regard.
RSVP	To respond to an invitation.
self-centered	Concerned solely with one's own needs.
socialize	Participate in social activities.
social media	Forms of electronic communications through which users share information, ideas, and personal messages.
staying power	Capacity of continuing without weakening.
sympathy	Caring about someone else's misfortune or grief.
tact	A keen sense of what to do or say without upsetting other people.

Further Reading

Lonely Planet. *The World: A Traveller's Guide to the Planet.* Singapore: Lonely Planet Publications, 2014.

Palepu, Hitha. *How to Pack: Travel Smart for Any Trip.* New York: Clarkson Potter, 2017.

Whitman, Beth. *Wanderlust and Lipstick: The Essential Guide for Women Traveling Solo.* Cleveland, OH: Dispatch Travels, 2009.

Schultz, Patricia. *1,000 Places to See in the United States and Canada Before You Die.* 3rd edition. New York: Workman Publishing Company, 2016.

Internet Resources

http://www.who.int/en/ Find reliable and up-to-date health information about every country in the world, including your future travel destination.

https://step.state.gov/step/ A free service for US citizens and nationals to enroll their trip with the nearest US embassy or consulate, allowing you to have easier access to travel alerts and emergency plans with your loved ones and US officials.

https://studyabroad.state.gov From scholarship opportunities to health and safety tips, this US Department of State website is dedicated to helping students.

https://travel.gc.ca/travelling A government website that offers helpful information for Canadians traveling to the United States and beyond.

https://www.volunteerforever.com Find out everything you want to know about the best volunteer abroad opportunities so you can travel the world and make a positive difference across the globe.

Index

Picture Credits

All images in this book are in the public domain or have been supplied under license by © Shutterstock.com. The publisher credits the following images as follows: page 24: Nuamfolio, page 27: SantibhavankP, page 28: Creative Family, page 56: Kavalenkau. To the best knowledge of the publisher, all images not specifically credited are in the public domain. If any image has been inadvertently uncredited, please notify the publisher, so that credit can be given in future printings.

Video Credits

Page 18 Qantas: http://x-qr.net/1Daa , page 28 PH Mountains: http://x-qr.net/1GoZ, page 34 TEDx Talks: http://x-qr.net/1FWw, page 42 Lavendaire: http://x-qr.net/1Ga2, page 48 soniastravels: http://x-qr.net/1DXB, page 54 geobeats: http://x-qr.net/1G2r

About the Author

Sarah Smith is a freelance writer currently living and working in the Boston area. She is also a board-certified Doctor of Physical Therapy, licensed by the Commonwealth of Massachusetts. She attended Boston University, where she earned both her doctorate and, as an undergraduate, a bachelor of science in health studies.

Sarah has been writing for her entire life, and first became a published author at age fourteen, when she began contributing to a weekly column for her local newspaper. Since beginning her freelance writing career in earnest in 2014, Sarah has written over 1,500 articles and books. Her work covers a broad range of topics, including psychology and relationships, as well as physical and mental health.

Additionally, she has over fifteen years of professional experience working with typically developing and special-needs children, along with their families, in a variety of settings, including schools, pediatric hospitals, and youth-group fitness programs. She spent over thirteen years working as a private nanny and babysitter for families in both her hometown of Yarmouth, Maine, as well as in and around the great city of Boston. Sarah also has experience tutoring and leading teens and young adults as part of a variety of clinical internship programs for physical therapy.